WHAT'S INSIDE A MOSQUE? PLACES OF WORSHIP

RELIGION BOOK FOR KIDS
CHILDREN'S ISLAM BOOKS

In this book, we're going to talk
about what's inside a mosque.
So, let's get right to it!

WHAT IS A MOSQUE?

A mosque, which is called masjid in the Arabic language, is the temple where those who believe in the Islam religion pray. The people who believe in the Islam religion are called Muslims. Muslims can pray in private and they can pray either indoors or outdoors. However, most Muslim communities have a dedicated building for prayer that is done in community groups. These buildings are called mosques.

MUSLIM PRAYING

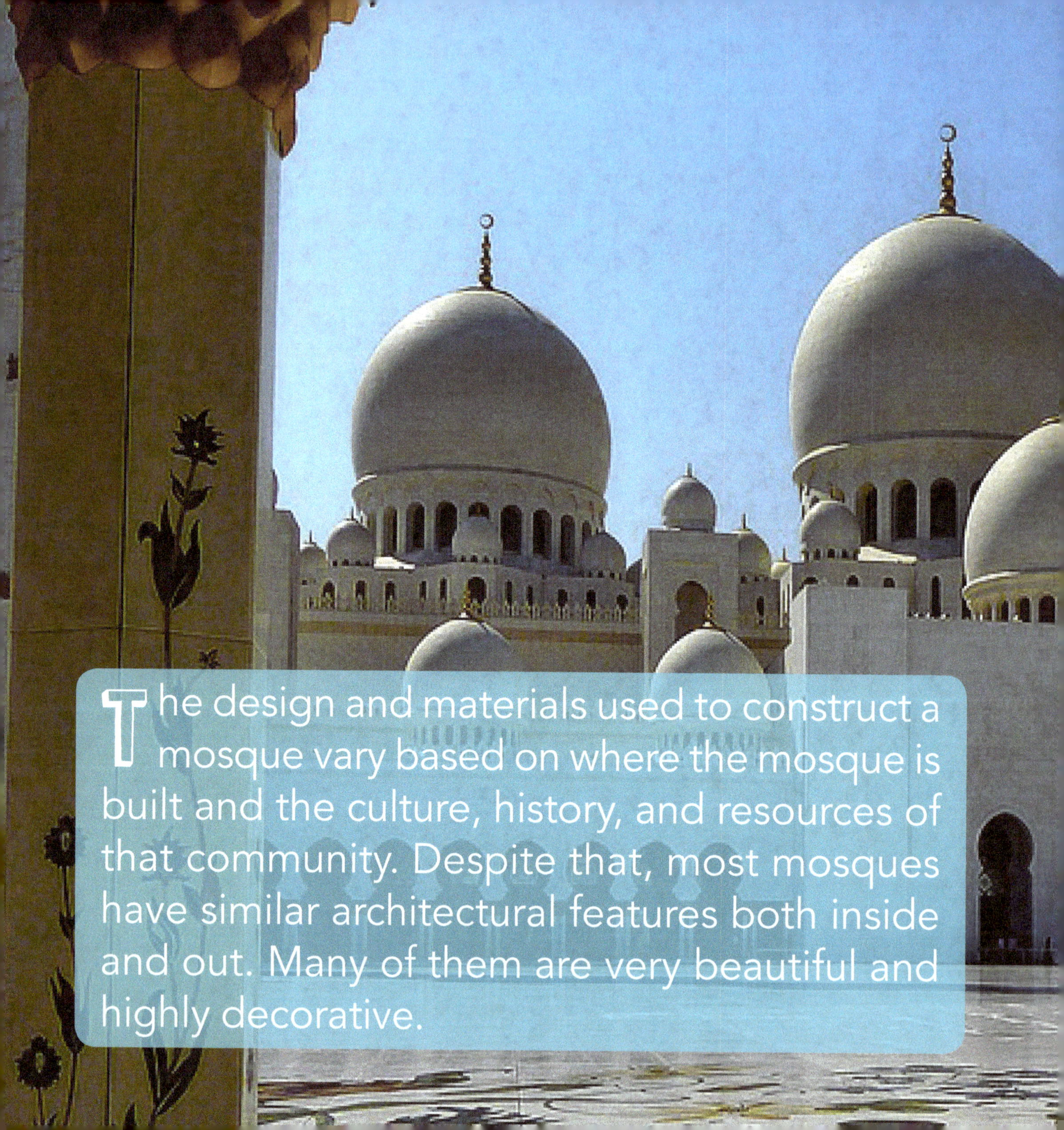

The design and materials used to construct a mosque vary based on where the mosque is built and the culture, history, and resources of that community. Despite that, most mosques have similar architectural features both inside and out. Many of them are very beautiful and highly decorative.

MOSQUE

MINARET

WHAT IS A MINARET AND WHAT IS ITS PURPOSE?

A minaret is a tall, skinny tower. It is a feature that distinguishes a mosque from other types of temples. Every mosque has a different number and style of minarets. They are sometimes square-shaped or eight-sided. Sometimes they are like tall, thin, cylinders. They usually have pointed roofs.

Originally, this is where the call for worshippers to join in prayer was sent out. This call is described as the "adhan." Today, microphones or loudspeakers are used to call the worshippers to the mosque. However, the traditional look of the minarets has remained a part of the architecture.

MICROPHONE

THE DOME

THE DOME

Many mosques, especially those in the Middle East, have rooftops shaped as domes. The dome usually covers the central core of the mosque, which is the prayer hall. Secondary domes are sometimes part of a mosque's architecture as well. The domes are usually highly decorated both on the outside and the inside of the building. The inside decorations have patterns with floral or geometric designs.

THE PRAYER HALL

The prayer hall is generally situated under the dome of the mosque. It is described as a "musalla," which means "place of prayer." It is a very bare space with almost no furniture. There are no pews like there are in Christian churches. Instead, the Muslim worshippers sit or kneel on the floor on prayer rugs. Sometimes there are a few isolated chairs or benches, but these are only to be used by worshippers who have a disability and can't sit or kneel for long periods of time.

PRAYER HALL

QURAN

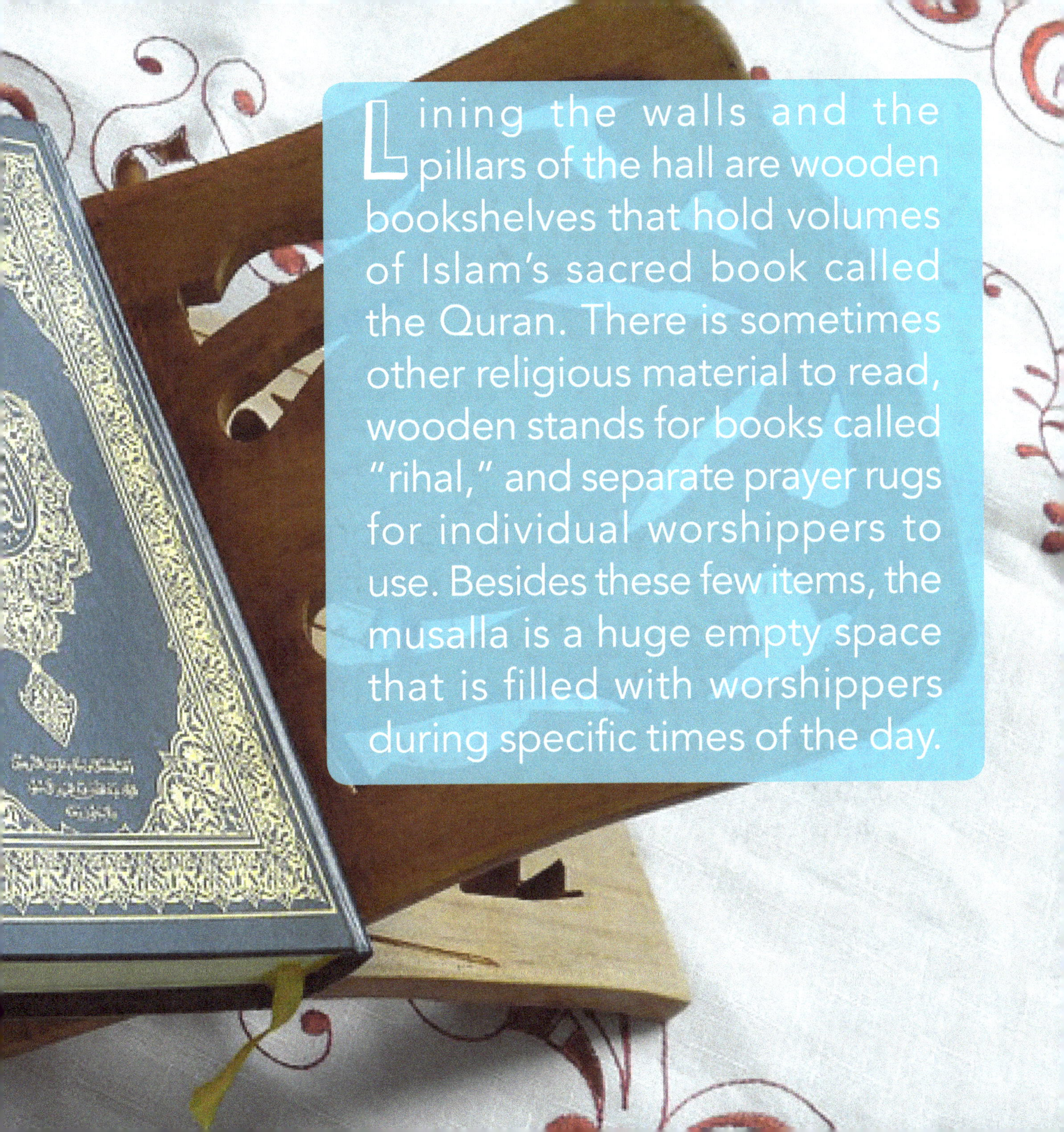

Lining the walls and the pillars of the hall are wooden bookshelves that hold volumes of Islam's sacred book called the Quran. There is sometimes other religious material to read, wooden stands for books called "rihal," and separate prayer rugs for individual worshippers to use. Besides these few items, the musalla is a huge empty space that is filled with worshippers during specific times of the day.

THE MIHRAB

In the wall of the prayer room, there is an indentation that is semi-circular. It is called a "mihrab" and it is highly decorated. The purpose of the mihrab, also known as the prayer niche, is to show the correct direction of the "Qiblah."

MIHRAB

MECCA, SAUDI ARABIA

The Qiblah is the direction that points to the sacred location of Mecca in modern-day Saudi Arabia. Muslims face Mecca whenever they pray and they pray five times a day.

The mihrabs in different mosques vary in shape and size as well as in color and decoration. Usually they look something like doorways and they are often adorned with mosaics made of tiles and calligraphy so that they can be distinguished from the rest of the space. The shape of the mihrab helps to amplify the imam's voice.

The imam is the wise Muslim who is the community leader and who speaks the prayers aloud during worship sessions. Of course, today, microphones also help the imam project his voice. Women generally have a separate prayer area inside the mosque and the words of the imam are televised to them so they can participate.

MUSLIM WOMEN PRAYING AT THE MOSQUE

WHY IS THE QIBLAH IMPORTANT?

At the beginning of the religion of Islam, the direction of the Qiblah was facing Jerusalem. However in 624 CE, Muhammad was told by Allah, the Muslim God, to change the Qiblah's direction to the Sacred Mosque in Mecca. The Sacred Mosque is home to the Ka'aba.

KA'ABA

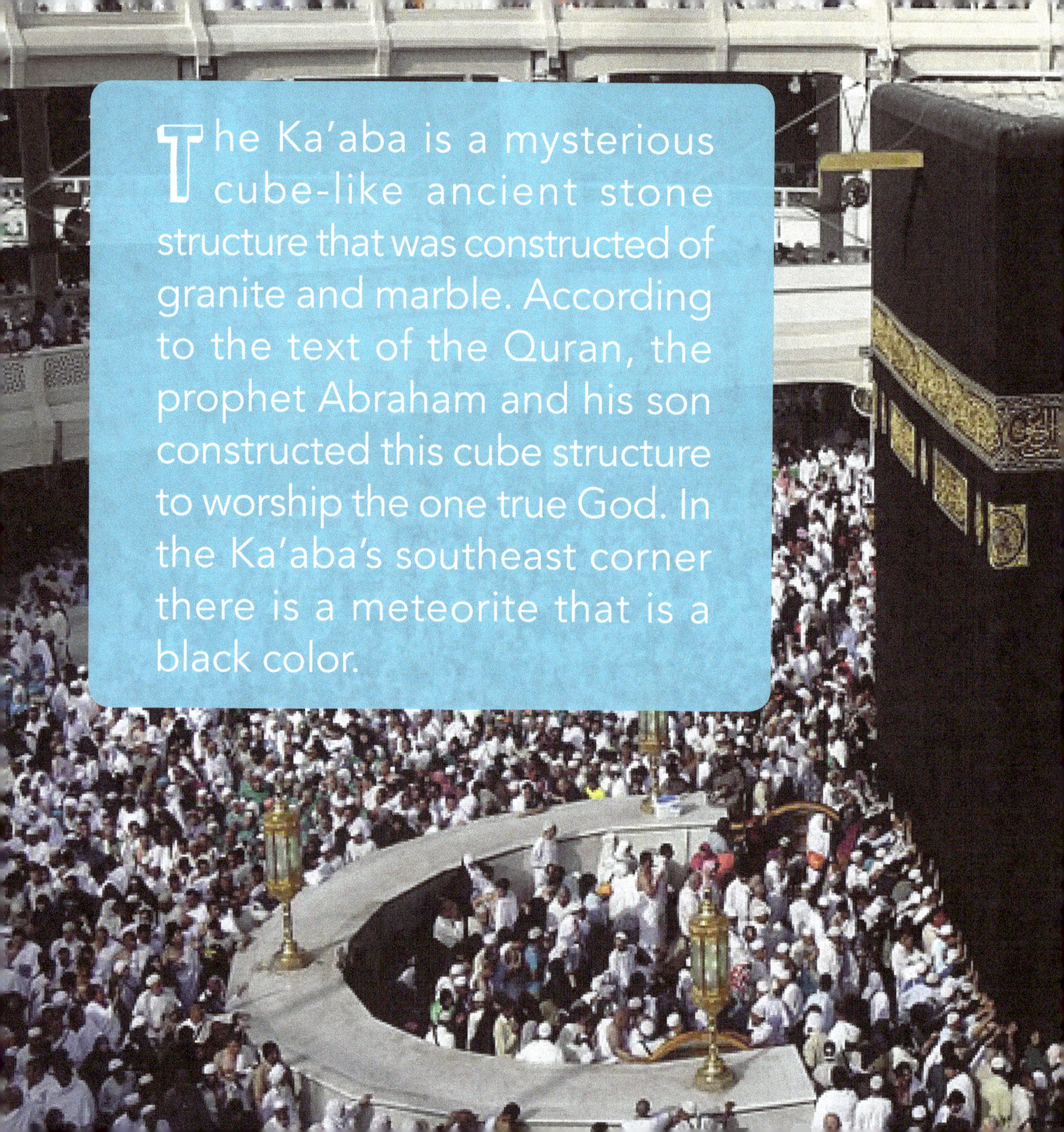

The Ka'aba is a mysterious cube-like ancient stone structure that was constructed of granite and marble. According to the text of the Quran, the prophet Abraham and his son constructed this cube structure to worship the one true God. In the Ka'aba's southeast corner there is a meteorite that is a black color.

There are many theories about this "black stone," but it is considered sacred and only Muslims are allowed to touch it. Some people believe that the angel Gabriel is the source of this "stone from heaven." Others believe that Adam was given the stone by God to erase his sins.

MUSLIM MEN PRAYING AT THE MOSQUE

Muslims don't worship the Ka'aba. They worship Allah, their one true God. However, having a Qiblah means that all the worshippers who believe in the Islam religion have a central focus and a spirit of unity throughout the world.

When it's possible, mosques are constructed so that they face the Qiblah. This makes it simpler for the worshippers to organize themselves into rows as they pray. Today many Muslims use smart phone technology to face the correct direction wherever they are. By simply typing in their address they can get the direction and the distance to the Ka'aba in Mecca.

MINBAR

THE MINBAR

In the front part of the hall of prayer, there is a tall platform that has steps leading to the top. It is made of wood or sometimes carved stone. The platform at the top sometimes has a dome at its peak.

This inside structure is called the minbar and it is where sermons are presented. It is located on the right side of the mihrab. The speaker is the imam and he either sits or stands at the top of the minbar's stairs when talking to the worshippers.

Originally, the minbar was constructed in this way to amplify the speaker's voice so he could be heard from a distance, just like the construction of the mihrab, but, of course, today, microphones are used to ensure the speaker can be heard.

THE ABLUTION AREA

Before Muslims participate in worship, they must go through a ritual washing to become pure in the sight of Allah. These ritual ablutions, which are also called wudu, can take place in any restroom. Sometimes inside or outside the mosque there are fountains along a wall with seats so that worshippers can sit when they wash their feet.

ABLUTION AREA

The ritual of washing is very specific even though only a small amount of water is used. The hands, mouth, nose, arms, face, and feet are all washed three times. The head and the ears are washed once.

THE PRAYER RUGS

When Muslims pray, cleanliness is important to them. The worshippers bow before Allah in humility. Prayer rugs have become the best way to keep a specific prayer area clean. They are used in mosques and at home. They also serve a practical purpose because they provide a surface that is cushioned.

Prayer
Rugs

Inside the mosque, the prayer hall is frequently covered with larger prayer carpets. The smaller prayer rugs are sometimes stacked on shelves nearby for worshippers to take and place over the larger carpets.

ost of the rugs have beautiful designs on them and have a definite "top" and "bottom." The worshipper uses the bottom to stand and the top points to the Qiblah. When prayers are over the one-meter-long rug is folded or rolled for storage so that it remains clean.

THE SHOE SHELF

Before entering the mosque, Muslims take their shoes off. This again is one of the ways that the mosque is kept clean in preparation for worship. The shoes are organized neatly into shelves so that when prayer time is over the worshippers can find their own shoes.

SUMMARY

Muslims believe in one god. They call him Allah. They pray to Allah five times a day from inside their homes or from inside or outside a mosque. Before they enter a mosque, they take off their shoes and go through a process of ritual ablution where they wash themselves so they are ready to worship.

nce they are ready, they go to the prayer hall where they kneel or sit on prayer rugs to pray as they face the sacred mosque in Mecca. The imam leads the prayers from his platform called the minbar, which is next to the mihrab. The mihrab is a semi-circular indentation in the prayer hall that points to the direction of Mecca.

Mosques are beautiful places of worship and they are usually decorated with geometric and floral tiles. They frequently have minarets, which were initially designed to call the worshippers for prayer, and domes, which provide a beautiful ceiling for the prayer hall or musalla.

Awesome! Now that you've read about what's inside a mosque, you may want to read about the history of Islam in the Baby Professor book *The History of the Islamic Empire.*

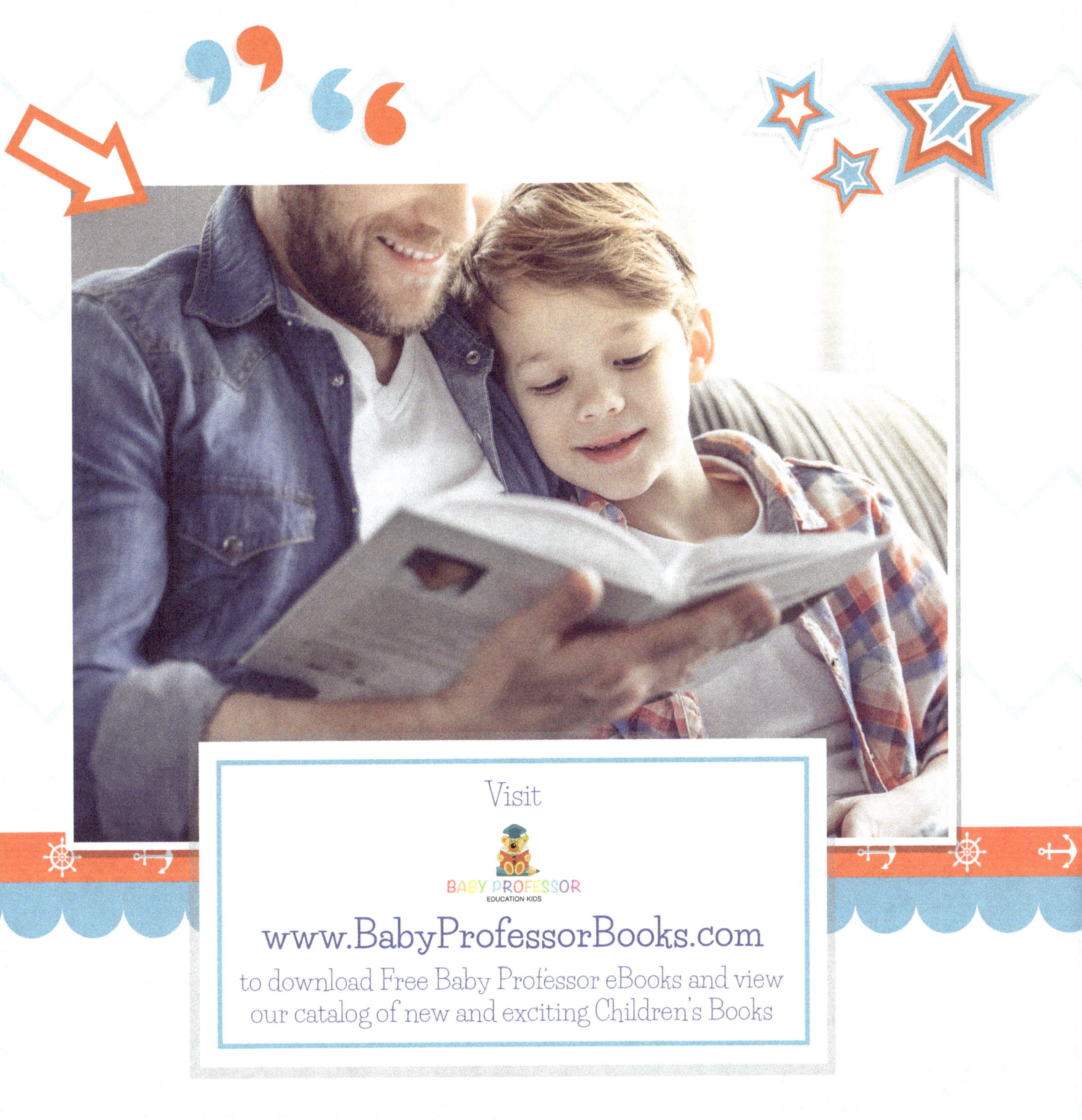

Visit
BABY PROFESSOR
EDUCATION KIDS
www.BabyProfessorBooks.com
to download Free Baby Professor eBooks and view
our catalog of new and exciting Children's Books